52 Tips For A Fantastic Year!

Simple Ideas - Big Impact

by
Adele de Caso

Printed in the United Kingdom.
First Printing, 2015

ISBN 978-0-9561473-1-8

Alenda Publishing
www.alendapublishing.com

This book is dedicated to my husband Jaime and my three children Sofia, Phoebe and Javier. You are my world and my reason for succeeding.

Acknowledgements

I would like to thank Robert Wilton for the cover design.

Barry Philips from Knowledge Is King, for his advice and endorsement.

My husband Jaime de Caso for his technical skills and constant support.

I would also like to thank Cadbury's for coming to my aid whenever I needed you. A Cream Egg never failed to get the creative juices flowing.

About The Author

Adele is a wife, mum, business owner and success coach. Her first book, Shy People Can Be Successful Too! - How To Achieve Your Dreams Without Changing Your Personality was published in 2009.

Adele came across personal development in 1996. She was a very shy individual with low self-esteem, but she desperately wanted more out of life. Having experienced the huge benefits of personal development herself, she went on to become successful in many areas. She now enjoys sharing her findings with others and helping them to achieve their true dreams and ambitions.

You can find more information on Adele's website
www.adeledecaso.com

Introduction

Within this book there are 52 tips to help you on your success journey. Its up to you how you use them, you can work on one tip each week or one tip each day. You can just read the whole book through in one sitting, the only thing I ask is that you take action on what you have learned.

They are split into four categories: mindset, confidence, goal setting and success habits. They are in this order because I believe that this is how you will benefit from them the most.

Mindset – Tips 1 to 17

I believe that mindset is the starting point for all success. Once you have the right mindset, you can implement new ideas and form new habits. You will have the attitude and the vision for success.

Self-Confidence – Tips 18 to 25

The tips in this category are going to help you to build the confidence and belief in yourself so that you can achieve whatever it is that success means to you.

Goals and Ambitions – Tips 26 to 36

I would not be where I am today and I would not have the things I have in my life today, if it had not been for goal setting. For this reason goal setting is very close to my heart. In this category I will share with you some goal setting tips that I have used to achieve even my most challenging goals.

Success Habits – Tips 37 to 52

Jim Rohn said, *"Success is nothing more than a few simple disciplines practiced every day"*. In this category, you will find some simple success habits to add to your daily routine and some success philosophies that will aid your personal growth thus allowing you to achieve your desired level of success.

Mindset

Tip 1 – Create A Positive Mind

I feel passionate about the benefits of a positive mind. What goes on in your mind makes all the difference, it affects your actions and your choices.

It is so important to separate yourself from negative influences. Make a decision to stop watching and listening to the news and reading negativity in the newspapers. Instead fill your mind with positive material.

When you get up in the morning, read for 10 minutes from a personal development book instead of turning on the TV. It will make a difference in how your whole day turns out.

Don't associate with negative people either; surround yourself with positive, like-minded people.

Positive thinking is a habit and will take a little discipline. At first it will be easier to set aside some time to work on this. By this I mean time for reading, listening or writing out some positive affirmations, for example. However, after a period of time, it will become natural to think in this way.

"Change your thoughts and you change your world"

Norman Vincent Peale

Tip 2 – Begin A Gratitude Journal

Gratitude is a fantastic attitude. Begin to appreciate everything that you have in your life. Keep a journal beside your bed and write down three things every day that you feel grateful for. (You can write more if you want) The things on your list can be simple, little things that are sometimes taken for granted on a daily basis. They could also be events that have happened during your day or lovely things that people have said to you.

When you have kept your gratitude journal for a period of time, it is really satisfying and rewarding to pick it up and look back at all the good things that you've had in your life.

Keeping a gratitude journal encourages you to go through your day looking for things to be grateful for, and guess what? When you do this they show up! That's not the only benefit; when you focus on things to appreciate you are not focusing on the things that you don't have. It changes your whole personal vibration. When you are grateful for what you already have you will receive more of what you want.

If you have children, I think this is a fantastic exercise for them too. You cannot start them too early! If you prefer you can use a gratitude jar instead. Write down things you are grateful for on pieces of paper, fold them up and put them in the jar. At the end of the year open it and read about all the fantastic things that have happened to you.

"If you want to turn your life around, try thankfulness. It will change your life mightily"
Gerald Good

Tip 3 - Doodle Pound Signs

This is a lot of fun and it works!

I first learned about this in a book called 'The Magic of Believing' by Claude M Bristol. The author would doodle on every piece of paper that crossed his desk and on the covers of files and directories. He even doodled on important correspondence!

I have always doodled, especially when talking on the phone and I used to do it when I attended lectures at university. I have now made it a habit whenever I doodle, to doodle pound signs.

£££££££££££££££££££££££££££££££

Achievement of most goals and dreams involves money to some degree. Whether it is for buying something material, charitable giving, or creating time freedom to make choices, money is usually required.

The activity of doodling pound signs is a fantastic way of creating a 'wealth' mindset. It's easy to do, doesn't take up any extra time, and is very effective. It is a deliberate form of visualisation, and it enforces your belief that you'll attain abundance in your life.

Give it a go......what have you got to lose?

"Every person is the creation of himself, the image of his own thinking and believing. As individuals think and believe, so they are"
Claude Bristol

Tip 4 – Be Happy For Others

Being happy for others when they, already, have what you want will help you to acquire it for yourself.

Never be envious of others, it will create bad feelings that will not attract good things towards you.

There is a wealth of abundance to go around, just because someone has achieved something doesn't mean that there is less available for you.

If you look at someone who drives past you in the car of your dreams and all you can think is "That's not fair – why does he get to be driving that and not me?" you will never get to drive the car yourself.

Simply be happy that what you want exists. If someone else can achieve it then so can you.

Allow the success of other people to inspire you and help you to believe that it possible for you too.

When you have dreams of your own that you are working towards, it will be easier for you to be happy for others. Start focusing on your own path to achievement.

"One of the sanest, surest, and most generous joys of life comes from being happy over the good fortune of others"

Robert A. Heinlein

Tip 5 – Eliminate 'I can't'

The words 'I can't' make you very weak when you say them and also when you think them.

Here is a very simple idea for you;

Take the words 'I can't' from your vocabulary and replace them with 'I can'

Every time you find yourself saying that you can't do something, switch immediately.

It will take some practice at first, you may need to display the words "I CAN' around your home for a while.

By telling yourself that you can do it, you will develop the belief that you can do it and subsequently you will take the actions that are necessary.

"Whether you think that you can, or that you can't, you are usually right"

Henry Ford

Tip 6 - Dream Big

Don't be afraid of thinking bigger. Everyone who has ever achieved their big dreams first started out by taking small steps. The difference was in their thinking. They had allowed themselves to dream bigger.

I think the majority of people have small dreams, which is why they only ever achieve small things in life. People don't stretch themselves because they would rather remain comfortable being 'uncomfortable'.

You don't have to limit yourself to what you feel is possible at this moment.

You also don't have to know how you will achieve your dreams in the beginning. When you start taking small steps, the next step will become apparent. People will appear, books will be recommended, opportunities will arise, all because you are taking action.

"There is always room in your life for thinking bigger, pushing limits and imagining the impossible"

Anthony Robbins

Tip 7 - Have A Positive Expectancy

Have you noticed that some people always expect things to go wrong? And then they seem surprised when they do!

You will come across people who say 'Oh why does this always seem to happen to me?' or ' Knowing my luck'.

People don't realise that they are actually creating their circumstances with the words they are using and the thoughts they are thinking.

So, if you get what you expect, why not expect things to work out the way you want them to? It's a far better way to live.

If negativity does creep into your mind, have a way to quickly snap out of it such as looking at your vision board or simply reliving a great memory.

"I believe the world is plotting to do me good today. I can't wait to see what it is"

Jack Canfield

Tip 8 - Take Responsibility

I first came across the importance of taking responsibility when I read The Success Principles by Jack Canfield. (A fantastic book I must add.)

There is only one person responsible for the quality of the life you lead and that person is you.

If you want to be successful, you need to start taking 100% responsibility for everything that happens in your life.

When things go wrong, don't look for someone or something to blame. Just accept responsibility. Blaming others just gives them the power.

Realise that you have created everything that has happened to you in your life to date. The good news is that you can create an entirely new set of circumstances at any point.

"People are always blaming their circumstances for what they are. I don't believe in circumstances. The people who get on in this world are the people who get up and look for the circumstances they want, and if they can't find them, make them"

George Bernard Shaw

Tip 9 - Carry A Gratitude Rock

Keeping a small rock or pebble in your pocket reminds you to be grateful. You can write the words 'Thank you' on it if you wish.

As you go through your day, every time you touch the pebble, think of something you are grateful for. You can start off with really simple things like appreciating things in your surroundings.

When you go to bed at night take the pebble from your pocket and think of something you are grateful for, and again when you put the pebble back into your pocket the next morning.

You won't need to carry the rock for too long before gratitude becomes a new habit for you.

Feeling grateful is a positive state of mind and it will really help you to manifest the things that will lead you to your dreams.

"The struggle ends when gratitude begins"

Neale Donald Walsh

Tip 10 - Act 'As If'

This is very powerful and also a lot of fun.

Act as if you have already achieved what you want. Pretend that you have reached your goals - you are successful in every way. Walk, talk, dress and think like the successful person you desire to be.

You can study the people who are where you want to be and start acting like them. You could get business cards printed for example, and dress like them.

Surround yourself with pictures that enable you to get into the feeling place of having the success that you desire.

Acting in this way will make an impact on your subconscious mind and bring about circumstances to make your dream happen.

"Once you make a decision the universe conspires to make it happen"

Ralph Waldo Emerson

Tip 11 - Surround Yourself With Positive Words

Words are so very powerful. Positive or negative they will have an effect on you. So, by surrounding yourself with positive words in your home and workspace you will ensure that you have positive messages influencing you in your daily actions.

Looking at positive words will cause you to think positive thoughts, which will in turn cause you to take positive actions.

I love to create a positive environment in my home. I look for framed images such as my latest addition 'Think Happy' which sits above the computer in the office corner. You can purchase hanging plaques displaying inspirational quotes or, simply just jot down positive sayings on post-it notes and place them around the home. Have a positive quote for your screen saver and make your password a positive word that will lift you up every time you type it in. Everyone in the home benefits from positive words, not just you, so you are creating a happy environment for the family.

Make sure you always have your books around you too, just looking at the books on my bookshelf next to my bed puts me in a positive state of mind because the titles themselves remind me of the inspiration I have previously gained from the book.

In the kitchen we have a blackboard on which to write positive words and quotes. The children love to get involved in this and I love it when I see a new quote that one of them has added.

"Every thought we think and every word we speak is creating our future"

Louise Hay

Tip 12 - Watch Motivational Videos

You can watch you favourite mentors on You Tube. Many of them will have their own channel. You can watch them doing live seminars, being interviewed on various TV programs or on training videos that they have recorded.

You can also gain a lot of inspiration from watching certain celebrities. One of my particular favourites is Will Smith. There are many video clips of him on YouTube where he is being interviewed on various chat shows; he talks about topics such as his worth ethic, the Law of Attraction and having belief in yourself. He is a very inspirational person. Set aside some time daily to watch, even if it's just 10 minutes per day. I like to watch first thing in the morning as I find that it sets me up for a fantastic day.

"I am still learning"

Michelangelo

Tip 13 - Listen To Uplifting Music

Music puts you into a happy state of mind; there is no doubt about it! It empowers you, gives you confidence and energy and makes you feel really good.

Sometimes there is nothing I like better than to go for a drive whilst listening to some uplifting music.

You can create a playlist of your favourite tracks to listen to whenever you need to.

Music enhances your creativity, it puts you in a feel good place and it can relax you.

Try new types of music to experience different types of relaxation. For example, I recently tried listening to some classical music and found that I really enjoyed it, but there are other times when I feel like listening to something more upbeat.

Whatever makes you feel good at a particular time is going to have a positive impact on you and your actions.

"I often think in music. I live my daydreams in music. I see my life in terms of music"

Albert Einstein

Tip 14 - Receive Daily Inspiration

Sign up to a daily inspirational messaging service via email. Many mentors have an email subscription service that involves a daily inspirational message being sent to your inbox free of charge.

Remember when you add more positive influence into your life there is less room for negative influence.

One of the ones I recommend is Mike Dooley's 'Notes from the Universe'. You can register at www.tut.com

"It's not what you look at that matters, it's what you see"

Henry David Thorou

Tip 15 - Watch 'The Secret' DVD

The Secret is a fantastic film about the Law of Attraction made by Ronda Byrne. It demonstrates that what we think about, we bring about.

Featuring interviews with many famous entrepreneurs, authors and teachers of success, it shows how you can use the law of attraction to your advantage in many different areas of your life. There is also a book and an audio version of The Secret.

"To bring anything into your life, imagine that it's already there"

Richard Bach

Tip 16 - Take Time To Let Your Mind Be Quiet

During my years of personal development, I had often read or heard people talking about meditation, but I had never really understood it properly, so I took some time to investigate it further, and although there are many different kinds of meditation, the common thread was that it was a way of quietening and stilling your mind.

It simply involves stepping away from the busy hustle and bustle of daily life to relax, recharge and enjoy the moment. It allows you to see things more clearly, and it allows you to benefit from important time where there is no negativity.

Now I understand it more, I can really see the benefits of taking this time out to switch off and clear the mind.

I prefer to refer to it as just taking time out to let your mind be quiet.

All you have to do is find a comfortable spot, somewhere quiet and just spend 5 minutes concentrating on your breathing. This will help to stop you becoming distracted with your thoughts. If thoughts do enter your mind, don't worry, just become aware of them and put your attention back on your breathing.

"The quieter you become, the more you can hear"

Ram Dass

Tip 17 - Make A Mind Movie

A mind movie is a slideshow made up of photographs, positive affirmations, quotes and achievements combined with an inspirational, motivating song track.

Mind movies make the visualisation process easy. Watch your movie a couple of times a day and the repetition, combined with the emotion, will have a very positive effect on your life.

Search for the things you want to include in your movie using search engines and then click 'images'. You will be greeted with lots and lots to choose from. You may want to use some photos from your own photo library, pictures of you with your loved ones or pictures of you doing something that you love. Include pictures of your achievements and things that make you feel good. Find pictures of the things that you want to achieve in your life.

Positive affirmations are also important and they can be found in the same way. For example 'I am happy and healthy'. If you have some quotes and affirmations of your own that you would like to include, you can make your own slides using whatever software you have on your computer and then save them as an image.

Next, find a music track that is going to make you feel good when you listen to it. It must be something that motivates you, inspires you to take action and has a sense of emotion.

You can put your movie together quite easily. Most computer systems have a program for doing so. If you would like to see my mind movie to maybe give you some ideas go to www.youtube.com/c/AdeledeCaso

"Whatever the mind can conceive and believe, it can achieve"

Napoleon Hill

Confidence

Tip 18 – Step Out Of Your Comfort Zone

Do something that makes you feel a little uncomfortable every day. This is how you grow and develop. You can stretch yourself just a little to begin with. Things that seem uncomfortable at first will become comfortable after only a short period of time. Your comfort zone is where you feel secure, but only because you have become used to settling for less than you would really like. Your beliefs have led you to where you are today, but by gaining some new beliefs you can move forward one small step at a time.

Regularly getting out of your comfort zone will allow you to grow and develop, and as you stretch yourself you will find that you can achieve more of your dreams and ambitions.

Your comfort zone is the place where you are free from anxiety and stress, your behaviours are pretty normal, there is no risk and you are comfortable.

This may seem like an easy life, but some people can become comfortable with being in a situation that they don't really like. It just seems that the easier option is to remain in that place.

Outside of your comfort zone is where the magic happens!

Surrounding our comfort zone is an area that, I will refer to, as the growth zone. Surrounding this is another area that I will refer to as, the Panic Zone.

The way to move out of your comfort zone and experience some of the magic that happens outside of it is to gradually make changes and do new things. If you attempt to stretch too much at one time, you will find yourself in the panic zone, where you will become highly stressed and experience feelings that may cause you to never attempt those things again.

However, if you just stretch into your growth zone, you will only experience slight discomfort. This will mean that you can return again and again, and you will become more comfortable each time.

Your comfort zone will become bigger as you stretch yourself and try new things. Eventually your growth zone will be where your original panic zone was!

"Life begins at the end of your comfort zone"

Neale Donald Walsh

Tip 19 – Focus On What You Are Good At

The things you are good at are usually the things you enjoy doing. Make a list of all the things you do well and do more of these things than anything else. When you are carrying out activities that you do well you have a great sense of satisfaction from doing these things. It is great for your self-esteem too.

By all means learn to do new things, but don't beat yourself up about the things you can't do well. Try and out-source them, your time is better spent doing the things that you excel at.

"Focus on what you can do, then do it with all your heart"

Lois Wilson

Tip 20 - Be Yourself

You can achieve your dreams without changing your personality. I am not saying that you don't have to personally develop. I am passionate about the very subject. But I do believe that you can be successful and at the same time remain who you are as a person. You can just become a better version of yourself.

People sometimes find it difficult to express who they really are, they hide behind a mask and never let their real self make an appearance. Low self-esteem is often the cause of this.

If you struggle to be yourself, just start to share a little bit of yourself at first. Then gradually let people see more of the real you. I think you will be pleasantly surprised at the response you will receive from people. You will be trusted more, and people will see that you are genuine.

Remember:

- You are running your own race, nobody else's.
- You can go at your own pace.
- You are a unique individual and what you can offer is unique.

All sorts of personality types can be successful. Don't hide yourself away from other people, go out and be YOU. If you don't, people will miss out on what you have to offer.

"Be yourself, everyone else is already taken"

Oscar Wilde

Tip 21 – Be Confident In Who You Are

The way you carry yourself and present yourself will make a difference in the way that people will treat you.

You are constantly sending out subconscious messages with your body language. Stand tall, put your shoulders back and hold your head high. Walk, talk, think and act confidently. Look people in the eye when you are talking to them.

Be confident in who you are. By all means admire other people, but don't be so in awe of them that you intimidate yourself.

Say to yourself; *'I am proud of who I am'.*

You may not be feeling confident at this this moment, but by acting confident, you will begin to feel so. You can pretend whilst you are developing.

"The privilege of a lifetime is being who you are"

Joseph Campbell

Tip 22 - Smile

Do everything with a smile!

Smiling releases endorphins into your blood stream that make you feel happier and more positive. What an easy way to change your mood in an instant!

Smiling has many other benefits:

- Not only does it make you feel good, but it makes other people feel good too.
- It decreases your stress levels.
- It makes you look approachable and friendly.
- It makes you more attractive.
- You will appear more trustworthy.
- People who smile a lot make better leaders.
- It is a very simple but effective communication technique.
- It is contagious.

"A smile remains the most inexpensive gift I can bestow on anyone and yet its powers can vanquish kingdoms"

Og Mandino

Tip 23 - Learn How To Motivate Yourself

There are two types of motivation, external and internal.

External motivation comes from things like attending an event or catching up with a colleague who, for example motivates us by telling us that they believe in us and that we can do it. But what if there aren't any events and what if we are working alone for a period of time? Who is going to motivate us then? Sometimes, the intentions are there at the time, but after the event or meeting, the moment in which we were going to move mountains has long gone. External motivation can be very short lived.

What if you could motivate yourself, so that the moment that got you excited in the first place could remain with you continuously?

This is where internal motivation comes in. It is the only motivation that we can always rely on. The good news is that we can do it using our own self-talk. Similar to repeating affirmations, you say positive statements about yourself, to yourself. They are not specific, they are general statements.

You are now the person that believes in you, and **you** are now the one telling you that you can do it.

Here are a few examples:

'I can achieve anything that I put my mind to today'

'I have the confidence and belief in myself to reach my goals'

'I know what I want and I have the confidence and ability to get it'

I recommend reading **'What to say when you talk to yourself'** by Dr. Shad Helmstetter for some more examples of positive statements that you can use.

"If you can learn to motivate yourself, you can always tap into an abundance of energy that will drive you to the success you dream of"

Rachael Bermingham

Tip 24 - Build Belief In Yourself

Belief is the basis of all action. If you believe something will happen, you will carry out the actions required. You must choose to believe that you can do anything you set your mind to, because in fact, you can. You get what you expect, so it makes sense to expect the best.

Hold positive expectations in your mind and believe that you can do what you really desire. A very powerful exercise is to pretend or **'Act as if'** you have already achieved your goal. (Refer to Tip 10)

You can also build your belief by:

- Reading personal development books.
- Attending seminars and workshops on the topic you want to succeed in.
- Seeking out information on You Tube.
- Reading success stories of people who have already done what you want to do.
- Repeating affirmations to yourself on a daily basis.
- Gradually stepping out of your comfort zone each day.
- Visualising your dream life down to every last detail.

"The size of your success is determined by the size of your belief"

David Schwartz

Tip 25 – Do What You Love

I cannot stress this one enough! Set time aside during your day or week to do something that you love to do, even if it is only on a small scale at first. If you cannot do the exact thing that you love to do, at least read about it or find some way in which you can get close to it.

For example, one of the things that I love to do is look at property, I am fascinated by it. So for a few minutes daily I surf property websites on the Internet. I find this activity really enjoyable and really relaxing too.

For you, it could be something as simple as going for a nature walk, reading your favourite book or spending time drawing or painting. Whatever it is make time for it. Look at it as an investment. Doing or thinking about what we love puts us in a very positive and happy state of mind, and when we are in this state we achieve more.

Perhaps you can reward yourself by indulging in something you love to do once you have completed your tasks for the day.

The ultimate in doing what you love is to discover a way to weave your passion into your work.

"Don't ask what the world needs, ask what makes you come alive and go do it. Because what the world needs is people who have come alive"

Howard Thurman

Goals And Ambitions

Tip 26 - Create A Vision Board

Collect pictures, photographs and inspirational phrases and quotes, and arrange them together on a board. You can use a corkboard or a large piece of card. Or you can simply stick pictures to your fridge.

The best way to approach this activity is to sit down with a pile of magazines and brochures when you won't be disturbed, and cut out anything that initially grabs your attention.

If you need some ideas of where to look for images, try home magazines, holiday brochures, luxury hotel brochures or fashion magazines. You can also print out pictures from websites.

Pick your absolute favourite items that really make your heart sing, and arrange them on your board however you wish.

Once you have completed your board, place it somewhere prominent so that it will remind you daily of what you want to achieve. There are many stories of people who have had images on their vision boards that have become reality. It has certainly happened to me!

When you have achieved something on your board it is best not to remove it, just either write in big letters alongside it "ACHIEVED" or put a big tick next to it. Looking at your successes daily will give you belief and encouragement and the desire to achieve even more.

Remember, you have to see your vision board daily.

The benefit of creating a vision board is that it constantly reminds you of your vision and ensures that you are always positive, because looking at the pictures makes you feel good, and when you feel good you are in a great place to attract good things into your life. Don't ever try to figure out how you will achieve the things you are putting on to your board. Just focus on the end result.

"Create the highest possible vision for your life, because you become what you believe"

Oprah Winfrey

Tip 27 – Create A Vision Book

A vision book follows the same principles as a vision board. You can use a scrapbook or a photo album. The vision book allows space for more pictures than a vision board, so you can fill a whole page with pictures connected to one particular goal if you wish.

You can update your book regularly so that you are constantly excited about new things.

The benefits of a vision book are that it is easily moved around if necessary. You can keep your vision book by your bedside so that you can look at it every night before you go to sleep, and every morning when you wake up.

You can keep it on the coffee table so that you can browse through it when you take a coffee break during the day. You can even take it travelling with you.

"Never give up on a dream just because of the time it will take to accomplish it. The time will pass anyway"

Earl Nightingale

Tip 28 – Display Your Written Goals

Something magical happens when you write your goals down. Research shows that you are 42% more likely to achieve them. So what if you not only write them down, but display them where you will see them multiple times a day? This gives you a constant reminder of the goals you are working towards.

Use post it notes to display your goals in prominent places, for example, on the wardrobe door, the fridge door, behind the bathroom door, on mirrors, even on the steering wheel of your car.

"The future belongs to those who believe in the beauty of their dreams"

Eleanor Roosevelt

Tip 29 – Write Yourself A Cheque

Do you have a monthly or yearly income that you would love to achieve? Maybe there is something that you would love to do that would generate a certain amount of money for you?

Writing yourself a cheque is a great visualisation technique. Determine the amount of money you desire, write the amount on the blank cheque (obtainable from www.thesecret.tv), date the cheque with the date you want to receive the money and pay the money to yourself.

Why not put a copy on your vision board and paste one into your vision book.

The actor Jim Carey did this when he was starting out. He wrote himself a cheque for ten million dollars for 'acting services rendered' and dated it Thanksgiving 1995 (five years later). He then put it in his wallet and kept it there. Importantly, he had faith that he would receive the money, and he did take the necessary actions. Just before Thanksgiving 1995, he found out he was going to earn ten million dollars for his film "Dumb and Dumber'. He then went on to command even more for his subsequent films.

"If you can see it and believe it, it makes it a lot easier to achieve it"

Oprah Winfrey

Tip 30 – Carry Your Goals With You

Write our your goals on small cards and carry them with you wherever you go.

Put them in your purse or wallet or a pocket. You can even laminate them if you like.

You will put yourself into an elite category of only 3% of people when you write your goals down. Look a your goals at every opportunity. When I started to do this, it changed my whole attitude towards waiting in a queue. It's now fun because I just use the time to look at my goal cards. How much time do we all spend waiting to pay at the checkout or sitting in waiting rooms? Use the time to your advantage.

When you write your goals down, you are sending a message out to the universe that you are serious about achieving your desired outcome. Flicking through your goal cards regularly keeps them at the forefront of your mind. It keeps you excited, inspired and motivated. The more you read out your goals, the more you will visualise and create the feeling of having them now. It is this feeling that attracts the things that you want towards you.

"Go confidently in the direction of your dreams. Live the life you have imagined"

Henry Davis Thoreau

Tip 31 – Have A Photo Taken With Your Goal

Seeing yourself in the picture with your goal makes it seem real. Like I said in the previous tip, it is the feelings that you experience that attract your dreams towards you.

You can have photos with your dream home, your dream car, wearing clothes you that you love or with certain people who you want to spend more time with.
You may have visited destinations on holiday that you would like to return to and already have holiday snaps. Use these too. The list is endless.

You can place these photos on your goal board, in your goal book, or anywhere where you will see them often. They will work especially well in your mind movie. Every time you look at your photos you will be reminded of how it felt to be so close to your goal.

I recommend that you go out and have lots of fun with this activity, and don't worry if some of these things seem a long way off. Remember what I said about "Acting as if" in Tip 10.

"People with goals succeed because they know where they are going"

Earl Nightingale

Tip 32 – Make Sure Your Goals Are Your Own

The purpose of having goals is to drive you and push you in the right direction, to enable to you to overcome challenges and to carry out your work when you don't really feel like it. For these reasons, your goals should be the things that create a burning desire within you. You want to achieve them so badly that you jump out of bed in the morning and can't wait to get started.

Your goals should be perfectly in line with your values and unique to you.

Are your goals what you really, really want? If you look at your goals and you don't get excited, they are not the right goals for **you.**

It took me some time to achieve my ultimate list of goals. There is nothing wrong with changing your goals as many times as it takes until you reach a list that makes your heart sing. Give your goals some serious thought, allow yourself time to come up with the ultimate list for yourself.

I recommend using Pinterest for inspiration and ideas www.pinterest.com. Here you will find thousands and thousands of ideas in the form of photographs and quotes and you can pick those that really resonate with you.

"The biggest adventure you can take is to live the life of your dreams"

Oprah Winfrey

Tip 33 – Create A 'Magic' List

We have already covered the importance of creating a list of goals or placing pictures of your goals somewhere so that they will be at the forefront of your mind. The creation of a magic list just takes things a step further. It is a list of absolutely everything that you want in each of your goals down to the very last detail.

For example, if it is a holiday, what dates will you travel and for how long will you go? Where will you go? How will you get there? How much spending money will you take? What activities will you carry out while you are there? Get the picture? Don't stop until you have covered every area of the goal.

I have made a magic list for the house I want to live in. It has details about the period, where it would be, what the approach to the house would be like, what colour the front door would be, down to what furniture would be inside.

Creating a magic list is a very special thing to do. It actually puts you into a place of feeling what it would be like to have it now. You become more passionate and excited about your goal and this motivates you to move forward at a faster pace. Create your list when you are in a really happy state of mind and believe that what you are creating will become reality. Your list will now have even more power.

"The future belongs to those who believe in the beauty of their dreams"

Eleanor Roosevelt

Tip 34 - Experience Your Goals

Where possible, feel what it would be like to have already achieved your goals. Experience what it would be like to actually have it now. For example, if you really desire a particular kind of car, arrange a test drive so that you know what it feels like to sit in the seat and hold the steering wheel. You will know how the engine sounds and what the interior smells like.

If you have a new home on your list of goals, visit the show-home. If it is a holiday that you want to achieve, visit the travel agent and plan the ideal trip. Bring brochures home with you and look through them often.

I can vividly remember the time when I visited a particular show home. I stood at the top of the staircase and looked down and imagined our children running through the hallway. A year or so later we moved into our new dream home.

"Desire is the starting point of all achievement, not a hope, not a wish, but a keen pulsating desire which transcends everything"

Napoleon Hill

Tip 35 - Have Goals In All Areas

It is important to have goals in all areas of your life. The different areas to consider are business and income goals, family and personal goals, lifestyle and spiritual goals.

If you have lots of goals in some areas of your life and none in others, you will not feel balanced.

For example, you may have a fantastic income but what is the point if you have no time to spend with your family?

Goals do not have to be materialistic, they can be experiences, and the memory of a great experience can last a lifetime.

Figure out what things are important to you in your life and base your list of goals around these things.

There is a great goal setting exercise in Jim Rohn's book, 'Seven Strategies for Wealth and Happiness.'

"Decide what you want, believe you can have it, believe you deserve it, believe its possible for you"

Rhonda Byrne

Tip 36 - Create A 'No Questions Asked' Account

I first found out about the 'No questions asked' account when I listened to my first personal development audio by Jim Rohn. He told the story of how a lady he knew had asked her husband for some money one day and he said 'What for?' The lady promised herself that day that she would never, ever have to ask for money again. She went on to become very successful.

This gave Jim the idea to give his wife an account in which he would deposit a certain amount of money each and every month for her to spend on whatever she liked.

Now, my husband would never question what I spent money on, but the difference an account like this makes is astounding.

Imagine being able to spend on whatever you wanted or give whatever you wanted without ever feeling like you had to justify it. You can spend the whole amount each month or you can save it up for larger items, it's entirely up to you. The key thing about this account it that it doesn't need to be a huge amount, it soon adds up if you don't spend it all every month. But just knowing that it can be spent on absolutely anything is very liberating.

I think that no matter what financial situation you are currently in, having an account like this can make you feel 'wealthy'. And feeling wealthy will inevitably lead to wealth in all areas of your life.

"That's the key to living your dreams: you must live them first, at least in your thoughts, in order to manifest them"

Mike Dooley

Success Habits

Tip 37 – Read 10 Pages Every Day

Read 10 pages of a good personal development book every day. Investing time into your own education is so worthwhile and one of the best choices you can make if you want to become successful.

Once I had completed my studies at university, I didn't really mind if I never picked up a book again! However, when I discovered personal development books it all began to change. I started to love reading again and I soon became passionate about it.

To start with you might find it easier to choose a particular time of the day when you are going to read. Try to stick to this and reading will soon become a habit.

There is a wealth of information at your fingertips. Simply look in the personal development/self improvement section of any bookshop.

If you are new to personal development and need some suggestions then I would recommend taking a look at the list of books at the back of my book "Shy People Can Be Successful Too!" I would also recommend taking a look at one of my favourite book websites, 'Knowledge is King' as they specialise in personal development books and audios.

The benefits of reading are endless. No one can ever take your knowledge away from you. When you read regularly you grow as an individual. You learn how to overcome challenges. You become inspired to achieve. You will be happier and you will improve your relationships in all areas.

"Many times the reading of a book has made the future of a man"

Ralph Waldo Emerson

Tip 38 - Listen For 15 Minutes Every Day

Listen to at least 15 minutes of a personal development audio every day. Instead of turning on the radio when you get into your car, put on a personal development CD and take advantage of this time when you can't be doing anything else. Most books are now available in audio format. The very first audio I ever listened to was a tape set by Jim Rohn called "The Art of Exceptional Living". What I learned from this audio programme has been invaluable to me.

The benefit of listening to audio is that it doesn't have to take any extra time. Think of the amount of time you spend in your car each day, especially if you have a long commute to work. Turn this time into learning time and you will find that you arrive at your destination a lot more positive than if you had been listening to the news on the radio.

"Success leaves clues"

Tony Robbins

Tip 39 – Repeat Affirmations Daily

The things that you say to yourself and the things that you think to yourself are creating your future circumstances.

Positive affirmations enable you to replace the negative words that you may often find yourself speaking and the negative thoughts that you find yourself thinking. They also enable you to create a whole new set of beliefs about yourself. They work by helping you to reprogram your subconscious mind, which is the part of your mind that carries out instructions without question.

An easy way to start is to simply repeat positive words to yourself, such as WEALTH, SUCCESS and PROSPERITY. Say them to yourself hundreds of times a day.

Once this becomes a habit, you can begin repeating phrases to yourself.

It is important to make your phrases positive. For example, instead of saying to yourself *"I don't want to be tired anymore"*, say something like *"I always feel wide awake and full of energy"*. The reason for this is that the subconscious does not pick up on whether you want something or you don't want something. All it will recognise is the word 'tired' and so it will make sure that you receive more of the same, more tiredness.

An affirmation that I love and have had lots of success with is this one from Louise Hay, 'All is well with me'.

You don't have to say your affirmations out loud, just repeat them to yourself. Once again, it's best when you first start to set aside times to do this. For example, before you go to sleep or when you wake up. Once you get used to it, you will find that it comes naturally to say your affirmations to yourself throughout the day.

"It's the repetition of affirmations that leads to belief. And once that belief becomes a deep conviction, things begin to happen"

Muhammad Ali

Tip 40 – Study

All successful people continually study success. When reading personal development books, I read them through once and then I go back and scribble notes in the margins and highlight different words and sentences that resonate with me. You will get so much more from the book if you do this. You can write down things that you are going to action that the book has prompted you to do. When you read the book again in the future your notes will be useful and you will be able to benefit from just flicking through the book and noticing the highlighted sections.

"Develop a passion for learning. If you do, you will never cease to grow"

Anthony J. D'Angelo

Tip 41 – Plan your day

This is very simple but really powerful and one of the first success tips I started to use. Before you go to bed at night, write a list of all the things you need to do the next day. Put everything on the list so that nothing gets forgotten and then get up the next day and start working through your list. Start with the things that you least look forward to doing. Don't put them off. Put anything that doesn't get completed on the top of your list for the next day.

A great thing about the 'To-Do' list is that you receive satisfaction when you tick things off. Also, you will not waste time pondering over what has to be done. You will know what to do so that you can just get on and do it.

Something else I like to do is to write out a 'Ta Dah' list. This is a list of all the things that you accomplished during the day that were not on your to do list, but they were important tasks that you carried out because they cropped up amongst everything else. An example could be that you helped one of your children with their homework, or you had to visit the vets with a sick animal. Unexpected things happen to us all during the day and when we can tick these things off at the end of the day it shows us what we are capable of fitting more things in if we really want to.

As you tick your items off your list say *"TA DAH"*, out loud if you wish!

"If we did all the things we were capable of we would literally astound ourselves"
Thomas Edison

Tip 42 – Find A Mentor

One of the fastest ways to achieve success is to follow the guidance of a mentor. You don't have to look far to find one. Many successful people have a wealth of their information available in the form of books, audios, videos and blogs. You can study their journey to success and do what they did.

You may be fortunate enough to know someone who has become successful in an area that you are interested in. If this is the case, offer to take them for lunch, and for the price of a meal you get to ask them questions and benefit from their expertise.

Having a mentor will be a fast track to success because they will have experienced all the ways that didn't work so that you don't have to.

Choose someone today, look him or her up and follow everything they do.

"If I have seen further it is by standing on the shoulders of giants"

Isaac Newton

Tip 43 - Look For Ways To Add Value

Use every situation you can to think of how you can help people. Decide to be a positive influence on people.

If you help enough people get what they want, you will get everything that you want.

Why not adopt a philosophy where you always attempt to leave people better than you found them?

You can look for ways to offer kindness and to add value in everything you do.

When you go the extra mile for people without expecting anything in return you will change lives.

Tell people that you appreciate them, pay people genuine complements and smile.

Living in this way is very uplifting and satisfying.

"We rise by lifting others"

Robert Ingersoll

Tip 44 - Associate With The Right People

It is really important that you spend time with people who lift you up and who make you feel good.

I learnt from Jim Rohn a long time ago that you are the average of the five people who you spend the most time with. This applies to your income too. Your income will also be the average of that of the five people who you hang around with most.

Have a look at the people you are spending most of your time with and ask yourself if they are empowering you or draining your energy.

To start with you don't have to eliminate people completely, just start bringing new people into your life. Still spend time with the original people but not as much as you did before.

Spend time with people who feel positive about their future, people who have the same values as you, people who inspire you.

"Who am I around and what are they doing to me?"

Jim Rohn

Tip 45 - Be Consistent

Doing as much as you can on a consistent basis is much better than having a splurge every now and then.

When you are not consistent you continuously have to start all over again and this requires a lot more effort.

When you work consistently on a project, you will create momentum and your work will flow much better.

A lot of the actions that will lead to the accomplishment of your goals may seem like small, insignificant tasks that will not make any noticeable difference if not carried out for a day or two. However, it is the sum of these actions compounded over time that will result in the realisation of your goals.

"Success is the sum of small efforts repeated day in and day out"

Robert Collier

Tip 46 - Take Action

In order to be successful you need to take the necessary actions.

Reading will be of a much greater benefit to you if you take action on what you have read. Listening to audios will make a bigger impact on you if you take action on what you have listened to. It is when you put the ideas into action that you will see the results.

Every time you attend a seminar or training event, come up with a list of items to action on your return.

You can also get into the habit of taking inspired action; sometimes something will just feel like the right thing to do.

When you set a goal, you may not know how you are going to achieve it at first. Don't worry; just take some form of action that feels right.

"By thought, the thing you want is brought to you; by action you receive it"

Wallace Wattles

Tip 47 – Begin A Success Journal

For as long as I can remember, I have kept a journal for jotting down things that inspire me.

Inspiration comes from many sources, it could be something you read in a book, a quote on a wall somewhere, a film that touches your heart, a piece of music or something you heard someone say.

Make a note of these inspired moments. Don't trust your memory.

Also make a note of any ideas that you have, I call them AHA moments. You may not action them right now, but when you look back through your journal at a later date, the timing might just be right.

"Be a collector of good ideas"

Jim Rohn

Tip 48 - Create A Twitter Account

Register on Twitter and follow at least 10 successful people. You can then receive inspiration and information from your mentors daily. You can even become interactive and respond to their comments and thoughts.

By only following people who have a success mindset, you will not be distracted by everything else.

If you are not sure who to follow here are some examples of people who I follow:

Louise Hay @LouiseHay
Success Magazine @successmagazine
The Secret @thesecret
Paul McGee @TheSumoGuy
Oprah Winfrey @Oprah
The Universe @mikedooley
Dr Wayne Dyer @DrWayneWDyer
Mark Victor Hansen @MarkVHansen
Jack Canfield @JackCanfield
Andrea Waltz @GoForNo
Richard McCann @ICanInspire

"You cannot change your destination overnight, but you can change your direction overnight"

Jim Rohn

Tip 49 - Organise Your Time

However you choose to do it, you will benefit from some sort of planner for your time. It may be a traditional diary, a calendar on your phone, or a wall-planner. Go with what suits you best.

Not having a plan is like driving from one city to another without a map. If you want to be successful you need to know where you are heading one day at a time.

Set aside time for specific things. For example, whilst writing this book, I decided that Thursday morning would be the day when my writing would take place. I would keep Thursday mornings free on my calendar so that I knew that it would definitely get done and I also knew how long the book would take me to complete.

I am also a great believer in having designated times for work and for leisure/family activities. Having definite work and family times and not letting the two overlap will be better for everyone. You will find that you get a lot more work completed in less time if you are not distracted, and you will enjoy your family and leisure time a lot more if your mind isn't on your work. Your family and friends will appreciate this too.

"Wherever you are, be all there"

Jim Elliot

Tip 50 - Use 10-Minute Slots

Sometimes we are so busy that we feel we cannot get things started. I have a lady called Claire Mitchell from *The Girl Means Business* to thank for this one. Since I took advantage of 10-minute slots, I have become a lot more productive. You can actually get a lot done in 10 minutes. Because you know you have a deadline, you are completely focussed on getting the job done. You can set an alarm if you think you might get carried away. 10-minute slots can be used for reading, doing affirmations, visualisation, putting a positive message on social media, writing a paragraph for a website, blog post or book, or it can be spent doing some research on something that needs organising.

When I first started out in business and was working full time, I did everything in little pockets of time. How many times do you sit waiting in the car when you are picking up one of your children? What about waiting in doctors or dentists surgeries? Maybe you can't get your computer out in these situations, but you can read or make a phone call.

Use the nooks and crannies of the day to your advantage.

"Success does not happen with one event. It happens as a result of many small steps one takes to achieve their desired outcome. Every day take one small step and watch the magic happen"

Kathleen Gage

Tip 51 - Share Your Knowledge

As your success journey unfolds, you will learn a lot and discover a lot. Be prepared to share what you learn with others, don't keep it to yourself.

Adopt the attitude of being a giver without expecting anything in return. If you come across books, videos, quotes or blog articles that have been worthwhile to you, share them so that others can benefit. This will help other people who are on their own success journey. You will benefit too because when you share your knowledge, you deepen your knowledge. Each and every day, you will likely have something worthwhile to share that could be beneficial to others.

Ways that you can share your knowledge:

- Sending an email to your friends, colleagues or team members.
- Sharing on social media.
- Offering to mentor someone who is not as far along on their path as you.
- In conversation.
- In your very own book.

One small gesture can positively influence someone's entire career.

"A candle loses nothing by lighting another candle"

Father James Keller

Tip 52 - Say 'Yes" To Opportunity

Learn to say **'Yes'** to opportunities that present themselves, even if sometimes, the task in question seems way out of your comfort zone.

My motto has always been, if it feels right, say 'yes' and figure out the how later on. You will know whether or not it feels like the right thing to do.

One of the first personal development books that I ever read was called **'Feel the fear and do it anyway'** by Susan Jeffers.

If you want to achieve success in your life you are going to have to do some things that feel a little uncomfortable sometimes. This is how you will grow and develop as a person. Just imagine how you will feel when you have achieved something that you were afraid of doing.

"If somebody offers you an amazing opportunity but you are not sure you can do it, say yes – then learn how to do it later!"

Richard Branson

"The best way to predict your future is to create it"

Peter Drucker

Thank you for reading 52 Tips For A Fantastic Year. I hope it has inspired you to start creating the life you really want, a life that you previously only dreamed of. When your desire is strong enough, you can achieve anything you put your mind to.

So why not you, why not today? Take that first step towards your better future. I wish you all the best as you begin your most fantastic year ever!

Adele

Visit my website at www.adeledecaso.com for more advice and free offers.
Follow me on Twitter @adeledecaso
Like my Facebook page www.facebook.com/adeledecaso

NOTES:

NOTES:

NOTES:

NOTES: